VOLUME 3

The Unconventional CEO· Strikes Back!

EVEN MORE COMMON SENSE BEYOND CONVENTIONAL MANAGEMENT THINKING!

MARIO PRETORIUS

First Edition, 2020

ISBN: 978-1-77605-667-5

Produced by Kwarts Publishers
www.kwartspublishers.co.za

Contact the author:
Mario Pretorius
www.mariopretorius.co.za
Mobile: +27 836412000
mp@valcapital.co.za

Yes, you can judge a book by its title!

Today's conventional mind-set needs an unconventional approach. Dare to be different and succeed.

The Return of the Unconventional CEO offers a wealth of business and personal experience distilled into concise, thought-provoking chapters. The book packs a powerful punch. Jam-packed with profound insights into today's business dilemmas.

A guide for up-and-coming CEOs, a reference for seasoned CEOs and once acquainted, a trusted friend to revisit annually.

Francois du Plessis
CEO Vega Capital, Pretoria

In the age of
information
ignorance is a
choice

Contents

Introduction

No-one wants to work with over 200 principles, but then again walking requires about the same number of actions which you will have mastered over time.

This is the third volume of my management musings and yes, you are being reminded of the common sense you already drip wherever you glide or trip in the water on which you walk. Nothing in these tomes should be Thor smashing the Earth for you; it should only be like the Huginn* the raven who whispers.

I might be scraping the barrel on ideas, lessons and plain common sense, I do hope for you're a-HA! moments when you spot the traces of your own salt stains– the blood, sweat & tears of overcome frustration followed by your sweet victory.

Go conquer some more.

Mario Pretorius
Bakoven, 2020

---

* *Huginn and Muninn are the raven who fly over Midgard and then whisper information into one-eyed Odin's ear. Odin sacrificed his eye to Mimir for a drink of the well of cosmic wisdom.*

MARIO PRETORIUS' BIOGRAPHY

So far my luck is holding out. I have spent a lifetime preparing for things that may never happen; the peaceful revolutions and the earth-shattering theories. On the way, I picked up an MBA from the Graduate School of Business (GSB) in Cape Town and attended some postgraduate courses at the GSB, as well as Harvard Business School. My working experience includes multiple-year stints in Oslo, Milwaukee, Toledo and Ann Arbor, Michigan.

My corporate life included the very large (South African Breweries), the large (Malbak Subsidiaries) and the medium. I have listed three companies on the Johannesburg Stock Exchange (JSE Ltd). Because, but mostly in spite of, my best efforts, I have succeeded in business in multiple disciplines as founder and owner, across various industries, from property development to telecommunications. Through the Junior Chamber of Commerce I visited many countries, made lifelong friends and acquired an appetite for learning and understanding. After I fired myself as CEO of TeleMasters into the Chairmanship, I hoped a restless soul would settle. Forays into multiple-country farming, marine diamond mining, (more) property development, data center building and a child-feeding programme means there is some life left in the dog.

My full bio is on LinkedIn and on Who's Who. You can follow me on Twitter here: @unconCEO. My website is www.MarioPretorius.co.za. Please feel free to contact me.

DEDICATION

When does enough satisfy the appetite? Clearly not yet – this 3rd in the series was an unexpected work when scraping the barrel of ideas was my fear.

Thanks to the enforced 2020 lockdown and a supportive coterie of fellow captives, more ideas surfaced. Immense thanks to my dear wife and the three joys, my daughters, for putting up with a head-scratching grump.

DEAR CEO

'New normal' is an insidious term that insinuates that what we're doing now isn't good enough anymore. In the pseudo-wisdom of gray hair, I call this out. Your principles and business practices have stood the test of time and viral onslaughts; the 'new normal' should probably be the return to the bedrock and the base requirements of good business. Hence this volume of unconventional ideas from the school of life.

Perhaps a few may make it into business school literature but that was not the intention; if any of these pages can help the blossoming of common sense and better business decisions, I will rest contentedly. Go out and expand the boundaries of your Empire, make converts of your customers and admirers of your competitors. You only shine once – may it be a long and memorable day.

1.

THE GAP

Apparently, I'm a Boomer. Yes, money rained on us – or, more correctly, we survived the odds of post-wars (plural), high inflation, regime changes, economic injustices, migrant surges and skeptical, petulant and remonstrative youth in the guises of Gen X, Millennials and Gen Z. Surely there's even more buzz words which will define different generations.

Why should we allow this to divide us in the struggle against creating a better quality of life, instead of together battling against the odds of rocketing Bolshevism, socialist laziness and Free Lunches for All. Hell, yes, this shows my opinion of those disparaging the victors and brandishing the stick of shame against the so-called 'ruination of the world'.

Our own '60's resentment against The Squares are more than vague memories and every new generation needs to pass its rites of passage to acceptance. Bear with the youngsters, humor and engage with those young minds who are short on ideas and who have even shorter attention spans. Let's make sure our grandchildren are not left destitute of ideas and means to surpass our victories and successes.

You will have an increasing number of these Young Guns (or Blow Driers) volunteering to take your entity into the future for glory and loot. Bear this gap and build your bridges for them to cross. They may find their own ways over the chasm too. It may be better than ours. Let's hope so.

2.

BUSINESS STRATEGY 'PHILOSOPHY' – ALPHA VS. OMEGA

You may not be familiar with 'Business Strategy' that is followed by the word 'Philosophy' but it can redefine results and redirect your strategy, tactics and the rest of the CEO tools. The Philosophy part means thinking about, and then state, the desired outcome in terms of often-conflicting timing and tangible results.

The 'Alpha' Business Strategy outcomes have sales growth, market share, profits, and share price as primary elements. Often the goals are unquestioned and their sequence of importance varies on the whim to the Ranking Alpha of the company – share price or growth? Who doesn't want to sign up to all of the above? Shareholders do and the RemCom judges your performance by these targets achieved.

A Pure Alpha philosophy lives and dies by 'them numbers'. It is efficient but superficial; it is short-term and deadly; it is generally out of your control, unrealistic and it's a poisoned chalice. It's growth *über alles*. If you miss, it is ripcord pull time and your landing may be very hard.

Here's a different philosophy on how business could operate. I term this the 'Omega' outcomes – margin increases, cash generation, dividend payments, strategic domination, focused client selection, operational streamlining and increasing the efficiency of your people. These denote a different set of markers and a deeper understanding of long-term success with a longer timeline.

Pure Omega lives by putting the horse out to stud and not just racing it. It revolves around getting the best reward for risk, not about confronting risk in the marketplace. In Alpha, sales have to be wrestled from someone else; in Omega it should best be cultivated instead of bought by incentives, price reduction, furious marketing and costly sales effort.

Paltry cash generation means either a squandering of 'investment' of quantum and time, or that you are flagging margins that attract ravens to a kill. Alpha is not high on cash, margin or buffers, Omega is. Omega profits are made more by controlling costs than growing revenue. Omega philosophy is toning down on the cost of growth for the sake of cash generation.

Omega businesses are grown by fostering and deepening relationships. Omega margins are made by earning trust and offering the perception of great value. Where cash flows in copiously from efficient activities, the value of the business will be solidified. Omega picks its *who* and *how*; Alpha is bent more on the *what*.

Where is your philosophical inclination, Plato or Socrates? What part is Mammon for the money and what part are you St Francis for good deeds?

Alpha strategy is good and is the norm but it can and should be augmented by an Omega strategy that may be the better business strategy philosophy in the long run.

Year on year consistency beats short term success, maybe you should consider ubering over there?

3.

ZOOMING OUT

The sheer flexibility of language astounds me – the descriptiveness supersedes what used to be our straight-shooting vocabulary. New terms abound and some are unconventional.

Taking in the big picture with a 'zoom out' seems like an occasional luxury, but it is also a beneficial necessity. When I chose to be chairman after firing myself from the CEO position, that was a zoom out. No more leading from the front but more a scout-on-the-hill. The perspective becomes revealing, the tyranny of hands-on subsided.

With lots of skin-in-the-game, prodding will be taken seriously. A chairman without company shares, or even CEO with no stake in the business, will not feel the same way about the future direction. Zooming out first looks at the recent past and then squints against the winds of change for the road less travelled going forward. It is more finding the path than goading the horse at gallop.

What must you do when your chairmanly sage advice falls amongst the thistles, and your ego is being mashed between a hard place and a rock? Zoom out with your General and revisit the initial assumptions – not your latest conclusions. Good coffee and cigars were invented for these moments. So sit on your hands to keep them from wanting to jerk the steering wheel to steer contrarily. You are paying a younger and more dynamic version of yourself to drive, and it's not always a smooth macadam road that beckons.

---

* *McAdam the Scot built the tarred road in 1800*

4.

CLUSTERING

There are many ways to describe bad sex, and one of those is a clusterf*ck. You might have noticed at the airline check-in that the larger the group doing the same thing – like checking in, going through security and meeting on the other side – the more disjointed and slower the result.

It's not that infamous 'airport gas' that activates the lurking moron in a passenger that suddenly cannot find the WC, it's how the group activity is organized. Whenever several people are tasked to do the SAME thing, the group reverts to the lowest common foot-dragging denominator, the leave-no-imbecile-behind mode of sometimes utter insanity.

Dictators were nature's way of saving at least some of the species. When armies move, even a *Blitzkrieg* can become a cluster of men and matériel. That's why sports evolved so participants have their own positions in the team. Tennis doubles can find both partners at the net, stupidly death-staring at each other with the "I thought you would' look, after the ball passed between them. Doing the same thing as someone else drags down the behaviour to the meanest standard.

Differentiate the tasks – it's all too easy allocating more people to help, and then finding the productivity inversely correlating to the headcount and to the combined IQ here. Wherever they cluster, trouble brews.

The Law of Diminishing Returns was probably born in a cluster of serfs, each wondering why they should work harder than the neighbour for the same bowl of gruel. If the outcome is not linked to an individual's own effort, there is no incentive to try harder.

The spirit of Personal Excellence is not invoked by the prospect of equal returns. Avoid the bad personal interactions, assign different roles, reward outcomes, or else they may not return to give their best in the morning.

Less clustering around is better for overall corporate health and for better conjugals.

5.

Collective responsibility

Article *33* of the 1949 Geneva Convention prohibits the collective punishment of civilians for an individual's misdeeds. This Convention, however, does not apply to your staff or to your children, even if they passionately believe that it does. Nope. Sorry. There are consequences when Group Think overrides company policy, common sense or just plain family civility.

Collective punishment can be of the stupid, untargeted kind – remove the coffee machine after one uncivilized soul failed to clean up. It can also be collective but clever. Revoking lunch deliveries from the take-away after the lingering smell of hot chips permeated the saliva glands of anyone with a pulse is a good move.

Can and should you punish collectively? Should and can you reward collectively as well? Imagine a conversation with your assembled Wagies*: let's agree on the same annual increases for all and the same annual deductions for all – that's fair, isn't it? Let's then use this leverage to individually punish – AND individually reward – shall we? This will be, in effect collective responsibility for individual actions as all will gain and lose.

Have second thoughts on this. Perhaps such an approach can work for teams, departments, or employees with the same responsibilities. How can rewards and disincentives be split between those with measurable outcomes and those who can only be measured by their consistency? It gets difficult to be fair to all.

Collective anything can be a mess, as the Soviets found out. Collectivization involves an abdication of personal responsibility, which is the cornerstone of maturity.

---

* *Wage earners*

Why hide behind or carry on the foibles of others? Some argue the Team concept is the glue for unity. This has merit – but just for specific once-off tasks or targets. Beat the Sales record this month; ship the Mendez order by Friday; or get collections under 14 days by April? Outperformance requires cash and accolades as rewards. Even rock bands split the gate by seniority, instrument, performance and songwriting contributions.

How do you escape the quicksand of the 'fair to all'? There is a minimum expected performance or consistence reward. It's called 'paycheck'. Whoever exceeds this requires the spotlight in public and reward in private.

What feeds the soul can be shared. What goes onto the pay slip is personal.

6.

TURKEYS CAN FLY

In the Cape Town suburb of Camps Bay, turkeys can fly – if the wind is strong enough. That's true everywhere: better watch out for the turkey and the elevating hot air. OK. I am pulling your leg! Even nonsense can sound like a wise proposal given the low calibration of today's BS detectors. Turkeys abound.

'WeTurkey' is looming in the minds of people as 'WeSpeak'. When 'WeThink' starts getting traction, the gullibility of the 'WeBelieve' generation may be curtailed. The absence of critical thinking in general is a result of the pervasive emotional judgment and personal feelings foisted on opposing views by an increasing intolerant academic and media communities. The 'ad hominem' false argument is played in an instant of disagreement.

Surely the WeWork implosion will be a 'Turkey' staple of Business School case studies for generations. What is the takeaway from this multi-country fiasco? Flying turkeys can cost billions in wasted capital.

Perhaps there's already a Ph.D thesis coming on the subject of the 'new economy' of disruptors, which should be dismissed with a three-word conclusion: "Where's the Cash?" The turkey of promise shall not pass Thanksgiving Day. Look out for these devil-in-feathers projects that defy gravity only when the fantasy of Levitating Air is blowing.

Jeffrey Preston Jorgensen had such a seemingly turkey idea and named it after a rain forest, but he managed to develop it properly, expand it constructively and it's finally generating moola nicely as Amazon. Jorgensen is the original name of Jeff Bezos, currently the richest man alive.

An enterprise needs to get to hyper-liquidity, or else it's just sucking cash and destroying lives.

7.

CLEVER, DILIGENT, STUPID AND LAZY

German General Kurt von Hammerstein-Equord's views on his staff should resonate with your finely-honed perceptions. Combine any two of these characteristics for a succinct description of your frontline forces:

Clever and diligent: Your frontline managers

Stupid and lazy: Routine duties and that covers about 90% of the staff

Clever and lazy: C-suite material because they possess the intellectual clarity and the composure necessary for difficult decisions

Stupid and diligent: Mischief makers – not to be entrusted with responsibility.

How about crude and insightful? We love to classify, to box and even to shoehorn others into our conceptions of Good, Bad and Indifferent. You are also being judged on a rather frequent basis, graded and pronounced-upon.

Bear with it.

8.

PERSISTENCE OF IDIOTIC THOUGHT

Blind spots come in all sizes – those things we see so often that they tend to get ignored. Think about the abundance of things that should be fixed in the world, but which we eventually end up ignoring.

Chemical poisoning of our waterways, the proliferation of illegal migrants and the surveillance state are a few such spots. Turning a blind eye to all these ticking time bombs, we still compound the problems by exfoliating our faces with microplastic scrub, employing undocumented workers, and offering our identities and mobile numbers and fingerprints to any boom-guard that asks.

Blinded to the consequences, we move on to 'fresh and exciting problems' like global warming. That phrase has gone stale, and it's climate change for now – until it is resuscitated into a New! Improved! version ... of whatever. It's the idiotic thought that becomes the blind spot. We still 'believe' in capitalism, democracy, equality, religion, law and order, justice for all – and those are just the main themes, per Ms. Congeniality.

Equality of outcomes is a Marxist fable of confusion with the real deal, the equality of access. A court can deliver a technical victory of law over justice. Religion is defined by its fanatical responsibility-abdicators as 'the only truths' – to be rejected on pain of death, by its adherents. Idiocy.

Beliefs involve idiotic thought. Does one 'believe' the earth is generally round, with flattened poles, or 'know' the verifiable fact?

Is *subjugation to a majority on the whims of uninformed populists* the way one wants to gain progress on the security of life and property? That is a working definition of democracy and the role of the State defined. Churchill called democracy 'the worst form of government except for all the others'. Anyone who has dealt with an elected body must have pondered that there has to be a better way to move the world forward. Espousing this cancerous practice of pandering to mass ignorance results in a persistence of idiotic thought.

Those who have served on a Homeowners' Association will have seen that democracy can be the shambles of the stupid and involves a lazy committee lording over the busy and the apathetic to the detriment of all.

The capitalists cannot define their system well except to say that at least it's not socialist. Free-market? Financial? State capitalism? Ditto with a Chinese flavour? It is idiotic to subjugate oneself to something so important yet so badly understood.

Too lazy to focus on the solutions, too ADDH to think it through to a more logical solution, or just too busy in a world of easy endorphins, we persist in idiotic thought against a hard and clear reality that should appear unambiguous.

Think better. Find better ways forward and implement something better than that which you know to be imperfect. Your world is one to be bettered daily. Stop the idiotic thought.

9.

Lovable rogues

Yes, they live and feed amongst us. They will fleece you gently and you'll feel you deserved it and you'll probably be too embarrassed to oust them for acting like the scoundrels that they are. Not every grandpa with itchy fingers and a slick manner is gunning to outfox you but a bit of inoculation is in order.

Lovable rogues endear themselves to you and filch your ideas with a thin-eyed smile. Lovable rogues heap intense love on you – for a reason. Thereafter, you are ignored again. That's the first hint that something's amiss: they are inconsistent in their attention. They will 'talk you up' to others as if your fingers turn deals to gold. This burnishes your-self-image and, man, does that warm glow last!

They then confide something to you, something personal that may not be true, but which could be slightly scandalous. Now you are in their trust. Looking deep into your eyes they innocently ask for that Deep Secret that you are protecting which will close the deal or seek details of the breakthrough that you plan to patent. Bam! Mission accomplished and you've lost it.

Take James. He is a slimy snake, bereft of morals, intent on structuring the world his way – taking the same trusting customers for a ride in sequence. Still he will no-expense-spared lunch you at Green Lawns and fawn over your every sentence as if you're the most important person to him, Most important victim more likely.

Any confrontation with the rogue is met with the same oozing love, tut-tuts and soothing admonishment to heal your childlike trauma. It will be repeated, if you let it. You need to strike back or you may strike out.

10.

Dangerous liaisons

Dangerous liaisons stalk the unwary. Many have tales of the 'I shouldn't have' kind and the debris of shattered careers are found everywhere.

She probably has the most intense blue eyes that have ever fluttered your heart, even a nanosecond's hesitation to dismiss her allure will put you in play. This Machiavellian power-player follows a simple and elegant strategy. She will gently push you to flirt, and when she's sure you're on board she will withdraw just out of reach and expertly maintain that distance for the rest of your dealings.

She knows that just wanting her once has made you vulnerable and she will consume you for that. When you're truculent she will get closer. When you're thinking in a non-professional way about just how she exposes that cleavage, she will play cat-and mouse with you. It will probably be hard to judge her actions dispassionately and she bets on that. She wants to get more than she deserves by giving you more than you can bite off.

Be on your guard when you meet the one that stares into your eyes from the first moment. You will not win this contest. Bow out right away, delegate the business to another of your own tigresses and stay alive. If it ends in a liaison, it will be more than dangerous. It could be career fatal.

11.

IF THEY AVOID YOUR EYES, AVOID THEIR SPACE

It is anyone's right not to like you, to avoid you or even to embarrass you. All of these actions have consequences and are often intended so. There is a number of wake-up actions up your sleeve to take care of the petty slights.

One clear sign of impending disrespect is a non-meeting of the eyes. Never shake a hand unless the eyes have already met, in a demonstration of mutual respect. The hands are clasped with the eyes in contact and let go before the eyes unlock. *Mano a mano.* If you greet someone and your outstretched hand is not met with visual acknowledgement, drop that hand, turn and walk. No need for that gesture to ever again darken your space and that outstretched hand can be safely ignored in future. Its presence may be noted with a very slight nod, while its reach can be ignored and repaid with a turning of the back. It's Fifteen-all in the game and it's still your serve.

Pettiness must be stomped out by elimination. Life is short and your dignity is important. It isn't a matter of pride, it's just good manners not being repaid. You can do without that.

12.

LINK THE REWARDS TO OUTCOMES: IF THIS IS DONE, THEN THAT WILL FOLLOW

Your mom did this very, very successfully. If you make your bed, then… This is linking a defined accomplishment with a defined outcome. So simple, so overlooked, so much wasted effort in getting tough things done.

Go link.

13.

People don't change

The saying that leopards never change their spots is quite true. Many sugar coatings later and still the truth prevails: wherever you go, there you are! No, people won't change. Not since childhood when those behavior patterns and coping mechanism for stress in the face of risk and reward were laid down, you should know that they won't.

Genetics is set at an early, debatable age – but, according to top geneticist Prof. Linda Gottfredson*, by the time you have reached 21 you will be 80% genetically determined by parentage and 20% by environmental factors – what you learned from parents and society. Your dearest and other co-suited people are the same, so is everyone down the rungs of that long corporate ladder.

Once a liar, once a shirker or once a complainer – that's the profile pic, the CV and the MO of the person. Although the flavour may change with the approach, words, manners, attitude, smiles and promises, it's still the same chassis, engine and gearbox. It may be a smarter paint job but they will do the same deal, tell the same stories, reach the same and – hopefully now well-expected – negotiating mistakes.

Habits are as stubborn as Lady Macbeth's damned spot; your hope and their promises won't diminish that. Sorry about your kids, too. But that's life. Stay away from the bad and the tempting; play with the straight and dependable. As a crop farmer will advise you: choose the seed with a consistent yield year-after -year, both in drought and in abundance.

People don't change and don't expect them to.

---

* *Professor Emeritus of educational psychology, University of Delaware*

14.

TIP THE CHEF, NOT THE WAITER

Who are you dealing with when you interact with the supplier or the client? Are you getting what you need or deserve? How will the waiter convince the chef to cook something exceptional on your behalf – unless you march in there and face-to-face it out?

With regularity some minion declares himself gatekeeper or a 'Mr. Filter of the information flow to the Head Honcho who holds the Yes power'. Without this appropriated and positional power, the hoodlum that keeps the door closed will be wearing a 'Help Me' placard at the intersection. He is battling for his job by keeping you from speaking to Mr. Chef. And yes, you wait. Job done for him.

Reconsider the approach and get yourself to the person who will actually use and benefit from your widget. Who has that 'skin in the game'. Ask *Qui bono* – who benefits? The standard approach is usually the correct opening gambit, but the outcome of business chess is to capture the King, not to merely wait for an opposing move.

Deals involve a number of interested parties that need to substantially agree to follow the one that shouts the loudest; 'yes, no or wait!'. Find the dealmaker or deal-breaker that holds the rudder stick. Go find and share tips with the Chef d'bureau. He should appreciate that.

15.

FEAR AND GREED

It's probably a line in a gangster movie or a Hunter S. Thomson quote, but *fear and greed* is all over business. It's part of the daily narrative. But greed is permanent. Fear can be managed by avoidance or be overcome by courage – greed cannot. Greed is in the DNA. Once afflicted, it is a bleeding itch, a hoarse driving whisper of the uncontrollable self.

The corporation itself is built on 'never-enough greed', with delusions that this trait can be managed responsibly. No corporation itself is greedy but its worker ants might have that hunger. That smell of success, the tokens of affluence and the benefits of swinging a Big Pair do not come from a fully ticked compliance sheet; they come from drinking blood from the skulls of business enemies.

The satisfaction of The Deal to Those Who Benefit at the cost of Those Other People is a thrill that speaks to the Greed alleles* on some people's never-get-enough genome clusters. Sometimes you may feel like having your Security calling the cops on them, but they are the corporate stars.

Margins can never be high enough, costs never too low, pricing never too predatory for the ambitious. How do you contain this, manage this or exploit the carriers of this mutation? Once you are called Solomon, you are the master of directing that energy into an acceptable model of mutual exchange of benefits, that is the original description of trade.

Pushing the limits should be for long-term gain, or else your community and the law might classify it as gouging, hoarding or profiteering. All these are seen as the curse words of lesser-success-

---

* *Alleles are the variant form of genes that determine the genetic expressions*

ful and over-prostaglandin-endowed weaklings by the Daedali** of your establishment.

There are unwritten long-term rules of the game that need to be heeded even by Unconventional CEOs. Sup but not gluttony, sip but no inebriation. Some moderation and restraint instead of plunder and pillage. In runaway robber capitalism you can Apple the prices until the backlash. Your choice – no tears allowed.

"Fear profits no-one" – an old Viking saying. Fear kills courage. Fear must be conquered by preparation and confrontation and repeats thereof when necessary to overcome it. Fear must be tamed and managed. Fear will keep you on your toes unlike complacency. Fear is an early warning system that you need and will appreciate; but which neck must be wrung before it consumes and paralyses your actions? Fear cannot be shown to lesser mortals but you must sense theirs and fortify them. It brings uncertainty and carves up the self-confidence. It can be as damaging as greed but in contrast, has an antidote; courage.

Tame fear and greed. Yoke them to your fast-moving wagon.

** *Daedalus in Greek legend flew too close to the sun in exultation, the wax in his wings melted and he fell to his death*

16.

ON BECOMING A CHIEF EXECUTIVE

That's the dream and if you're not yet cornering the Corner Office, here are some hints. In the days of yore, the General Manager ran the show for the owners, and everyone with a fancier suit than him were the Yes-Men, kissing the hand of the *Principio*. Short or rolled-up sleeves literally denoted him and the smoocher was almost never a hairy-chester, involved deep down into the pit of alligators of the money machine like him.

That GM had to know an extraordinary amount of detailed how-to's as he was the real go-to guy. Needed nuts? Get them there. Trucks on fire? Do this. Customers unhappy? Do that. The 'do-dis, do-dat' knowledge came from years of spannering the internal workings. GMs came up the ranks. GMs didn't jump ship for money. GMs had the balls to face up to the Idea Men from Upstairs. He batted for 'his people'. He was invariable right, correct, trusted and the lynchpin around which the universe swung in quiet satisfaction.

He had to separate BS from real threats and therefore had to know detail, lots of detail, all the detail and to know it across all the disciplines. He could spot discount mistakes on invoices, catch a delivery of the wrong transmission oil before the Goods Received Voucher was signed. He knew that Pete's kid was playing up again – and a comforting word there saved the project. He should be enshrined with a statue – the embodiment of the Spirit of Business, like the bonnet ornament of a vintage Rolls.

Except that the GM was generally considered too gruff to be allowed to politely shuffle the Board Papers while sagely nodding to the Chairman. He didn't make it to the Board and shrugged it off – that pansy thing was what Graduates sucked up to and insisted that the Real Power was his. He was perfectly correct in this too.

His Bosses came and went, a-hopping the ladder of opportunity, and he stoically faced down their forever-changing recipes from Business School. He ground them down, knowing that the real institutional knowledge rested safely behind his penetrating eyes and, sadly, would never be duplicated or passed on as GM's were a dying breed.

Here's the lesson: you have to be the polished version of That Man. The prerequisite for success is to get into and stay in the race. Your grasp of detail and an understanding of the implications of decisions taken every moment across the breadth of the organization is that will burnish your image of strong enough to lead the troops on assault and polished enough to stand on the bridge as Captain for the owners.

Rule One is that you need to understand why, how and thanks to whom things continue to tick over well and to grasp this in many decimals. You're faced with an army of specialists in their positions, but only a handful are the key men that are virtually irreplaceable. Ask, observe, and then mentally put together the 3D Meccano set of this Empire, and keep filling the empty spaces.

It is the generalist that will succeed in understanding the subtleties. To be considered for contention at the top you need Rule Two: wear-out your shoes in traipsing to the frontlines, accumulating understanding and scattering the fairy dust of your genuine people concerns. It's always a trust thing to get to the top, and genuine familiarity at the stopes will help your insights.

Your competition for Top Dog will generally stick to what they know: the Finance contender is digging for more suspect journal entries, Sales master is chipping away at long-outstanding quotes, and Mr. Engineering is rummaging around the stores for more reusable parts. You, Hannibal, need to be the unifying force of communal knowledge. Go wide and go deep; then share the insights. Strange, but your competitors won't ever steal your ideas to repeat or claim them.

Rule Three: those that do the selection must constantly be reminded that you are the old-style GM reincarnate – 'know much and do lots'.

Once at that pinnacle carpet you can plumb its depth – and its height of your quest for understanding. You have practiced being good at that and those now smiling at you from behind the desks and workbenches will have learned to be open and straight with you.

17.

ON BECOMING THE CHIEF EXECUTIVE – *CONTINUED*

There are many paths to the summit, the narrow and the wide abound. The twisty road in the prior chapter is idealized – but a solid pointer. Stealth, gangsterism, dead man's shoes, nepotism and plain sucking up have worked in the past, as have threats, acquisitions, lies and paving your way to the top by favours and bribes. Fame and fortune play their hands for the lucky and the brave. Your ascent is unique.

You have mastered the absorption of knowledge, sieved it through your academic training, spotted the inefficiencies and weak links and now you're an unguided missile that may destroy the Mothership. These glaring frailties all result from human decisions – or indecisions – and you know who's responsible, accountable and hiding in plain sight.

Like a wounded hyena staring down a hungry lion, the incumbents and overlooked will fight you singularly and in teams for the prize. You will face manufactured issues. What are the consequence of the impairment oversight by Michael's finance people that he knowingly overlooked? How will confronting Jan about the 'spare stock' larded away and off-balance-sheet for the engineering emergencies play out? Then there's Shane's preference for the blondes in the sales team and all the other inefficiencies they think the Old Man doesn't suspect.

Playing corporate politics is a PhD-level activity in itself and certain personal traits are more catalytical in generating benefit for the player. Firstly, you need to distinguish between what to share and what you would be wise to shut-up about. Share the good stuff, but analyse what should be dodged for now and formulate your solutions.

Secondly, you need always to play both sides at all times. You need to praise your colleagues to your King. You need to let the Crown know, too, that there are perhaps some chinks in the overall armour that are unnecessary weak. It's not personal; you are paid for doing a professional job. Boosting the balance sheet by inclusion of written-down but workable stock is a sound proposal, but you must point out to Jan that asset concealment will not sit well in his career plan.

You need to be trusted with whatever secrets cross your roving mind, but you need to know which of these are critical to the future of whoever it is that you owe your allegiance to. You are not playing in isolation as an up-coming pretender. The other candidates are doing the same to you. Out-performing others is not enough, out-maneuvering, out-profiling and out-politicking them are needed.

Be aware that internal company success is not guaranteed to get THAT title printed on the new business card. There are roving bands of professional suckers-up that may out-promise you to the Selection Committee from their vantage point of being a CE of another entity. In a world where CVs run to gigabytes, such an imposter has the dual advantage of promising experience and adding novelty in the form of New! Improved! and Fresh! ways of shooting the lights out.

You, on the other hand, must practice performing the coveted role daily. Don't be a smart-arse about your knowledge and insights. Keep your comments, suggestions and (if asked) advice practical, implementable and always targeted at the greater good, not just for of the benefit of department and the Ego who death-grips its reins.

If you are overlooked or sidelined without the Main Man's protection – it may be time to reach for the stars elsewhere. Your training makes you worth it.

18.

PROJECT YOUR GRAVITAS

What inspires people to take up arms or to lay them down? How could a lame Roosevelt, a drunkard Churchill or a heartless Stalin lead their nations? A lack of nominated alternatives is one good answer. But to be successful they, and you, need to embody gravitas. You need to project unwavering confidence to ensure unstoppable outcomes and to make unquestionable utterances.

You had better mean what you say the first time, as there is no room for 'misspoke', 'wrong interpretation' or 'misunderstanding the intended message'. You have one chance only – every time you open your mouth. That's unfair but that's the rule – the C Suite is not playing 'clarification' games. There must be a furrowed brow behind your smile, like Reagan; a deadliness of purpose behind the deadpan, like Putin.

In short: *gravitas* is a Roman virtue along with *pietas, severitas, disciplina, dignitas* and *virtus** – the attributes that made a good citizen. It denotes substance and responsibility. You may have missed out on being Head Boy but the one who was appointed may now work for you in accounts. You have to be Principal and House Master, leader and disciplinarian. You are the unspoken Rule Maker.

Whenever in doubt, your loyalists need only ask themselves what YOU would do – and so succeed. If they don't or cannot, you are not getting the message through yet. You must make Gravitas your project and then project it. The rule of thumb is that the further into the future you can set their sights, the more granite they will perceive in your image.

---

* *Dutifulness, self-control, self-discipline, self-worth, excellence*

19.

Unreasonable demands

Unreasonable demands question your power and your leadership. The proposer is challenging you in a game of brinkmanship. If you cannot meet that challenge, you could be seen as having failed and he knows that, hence the demand. You're smarter than that and will have developed a nose for odious schemers. You won't accept unreasonableness, even if it's disguised as a free lap dance with side benefits.

At the first whiff of such potential professional suicide you must gently prod with a purring counter-question, requesting detail. You may respond by 'Is that not unreasonable in the circumstances?' If acquiescence or detail is not forthcoming and does not lead to a back-down, your next set of questions will gently enquire what the impact will be on other departments – and you will phrase it in such a way that only you can know the answer.

Only the brave or foolish schemer will walk into that snare and the chances are it will be the latter. You only have to defend, and that's disproportionally easier than mounting a killer attack. Let the jaws close gently on that turkey.

You can wield soft power – giving a chance to back down but to make sure they understand that you can hurt them if you choose. Once they are subdued, follow up with a demand of your own that will take some strain to meet, maybe they must come and present an analysis of the changes on product margins over the last five years, by the way, that's due on Monday (always say it's due after the week-end). It's a direct order, so not executing it would be a dereliction of duty, a show of contempt or insubordination. Take your time to pick the appropriate charge.

20.

INTOLERANCE OF INTOLERANCE

A number of new beliefs are being foisted with great success and they lead to great destruction. Catering for the fringes can be an excellent way of identifying and filling a market gap, but it's not a good idea if it then upends your main market. Tolerance keeps the status quo steady. Big changes require intervention, not incrementals.

The intolerant one can become the champion by pushing his agenda and ideas. So far, so good, for your internal working – but in the marketplace, this can create slippery pavement ice. Halaal food and Kosher certification rules are examples of intolerance pushed on a majority who make wake up to find they are infringing their own dietary prohibitions.

Should these intolerants be accommodated or treated with intolerance? The accommodation of the single or minority demander – for things like transgender pronouns or BPO-free water dispensers – can be challenging, as these are aimed squarely at your empathy button. Resist and retreat. Special favours can be traps and precedent-setting deviations from common sense.

Yes, we now have smoke-free offices and Ally McBeal genderless toilets – but where do you draw the line on working with earphones, facial tattoos, comfort pets and a host of newbies you may feel under pressure to succumb to for the sake of office peace? Of course, you may discriminate against people – as long as it's not unfair. Thereby hangs the Claymore mine*. So set out a policy of intolerance of the intolerant. And good luck.

---

* Claymore mine is an lethal anti- personnel device

21.

STATUS

Pulling up at the office in the Porsche can convey either ambition or decadence. Either way it denotes status in the same way the rented Corolla does. It is a palpable symbol and signal to melt the social filters. Often the car is the object of desire and it's not conducive to the status of the man behind the wheel.

The status bullseye is when they want to have *that* car because *you* drive it, as my father Willem taught me. Gender roles revolve around status and no amount of *wimmin* shouting to shut the debate will change it. These lines are not composed to please the reader, but to remind and re-ignite the common sense you have – discarding the PC and drivel that demand conformity of thought and attitude.

Life is Darwin and common sense is Lindy*, as the risk philosopher Taleb describes it. Women are sex symbols to men. That's what attracts the boys. Wearing a pencil skirt, stilettos and a severe pullback to the boardroom doesn't *mannify* her. The boys only pretend it does. The ladies need to de-sexualize to keep attention riveted on the matter under discussion.

Men are Success Symbols to women. That's what attracts the girls too. It follows that the man's success status determines the attached woman's. Either she moves up to become Mrs. Clooney or moves downwards to being ex-Duchess of Sussex. Harry doesn't move away from his status; he IS his status and Mrs. Windsor gravitates there to enjoy it.

Why this explanation? Despite the pressure to equalize, include, diversify and un-male and de-sex the corporate world, nature won't be fooled. Despite your finer *mores* spiraling towards the gender-blind treatment, your coarser nature won't be overridden. Women know what they *don't want* and will settle on available choices; men

---

* *Lindy effect: the longer something has lasted, the longer it will last into the future*

know what they do *want* and they won't settle for lesser choices. This is a significant difference in approach and must be kept in mind. They're not better or worse approaches, but significantly different. Understand the 'his status' concept and be careful in this oft-offended world not to cause unnecessary trouble with those who stare blindly and angrily ahead through the blinkers.

22.

THINK PEOPLE AND DO PEOPLE

It is a sad indictment on a cruel world that not everyone can have brilliant ideas and follow them up with earth-shattering implementation. Ideas and execution traits are generally uncorrelated, unconnected and opposing forces.

For eons, the thinker/planner/schemer has lorded over Mr. Make-It-Happen and his brethren, and often unfairly so. When Genghis got the westwards itch, at least he rode in the front ranks and supped from a wooden bowl with his golden horde. Ditto the Great Alexander, and so on until some wetnose decided that getting mud on his booties would spoil his look.

Since then, Generals fought from safe command posts and deep Cheyenne Mountain bunkers. When was the last time a C-suiter sat unchaperoned across your desk elevator pitching his company wares?

The modern warfare principle since Napoleon has been for Lord Cardigan, (the jersey), commanded Lord Raglan, (the sleeve), sent up the creek with his Light Brigade towards the Russians at Balaklava, (the headgear), for just for a memorable Tennyson poem about the Charge of that brave lot. Did any of those culprits get a bad Performance Review? No, they blamed Lord Lucan, who thankfully had no sartorial elements named after him. The dead heroes had no say.

This disconnect between ideas and their consequences plague us endlessly, but it is overlooked as normal in business. A purchase clerk ordered the inferior O-ring from its manufacturer Morton Thiokol and boom went the shuttle Challenger. No lynching's followed.

Lucky for you the ideas people have a better chance in life; we are such optimistic creatures that we would rather believe a PowerPoint promise than a PERT Project Management reality chart. You're pitching to dreamers who view delegation as the 'doing'. Their shirt-sleeves stay down.

You, Sisyphus* on the other hand, understand the necessity of overcoming the futile and then uniting thought and action leading from the front as well as shouldering any blame – while letting the lesser generals share the frothy headiness of victory.

Then again it would be a hard roll of a rock up the hill to get your best doers to think creatively, but that is your challenge. As for getting the cerebrally inclined to dirty their fingernails in trenches, such lessons of accountability can be both callus-forming and cal-lousness reducing.

Close the gap: listen to the worker's ideas and task the thinker with a bit of back-bending.

---

* *Sisyphus was condemned for eternity to roll a boulder up a hill only for it to roll down every time – punishment for his deceitfulness*

23.

SLACK

How much slack is in an economy? Besides the snigger that the 55% of GDP of the Government, Public and Municipal sector is 100% slack, it is a question that needs validating.

How many productive hours are there in your, and in everyone's day? How many such useful hours should be expected, and what do we mean by 'productive'? If the Insta, Twitter, FB, smoke and comfort breaks, lunches, coffees, and personal phone calls are added to the unnecessary emails, browsing, copying, finding, filing, arranging and meetings, it may seem that there is little else left but to stare a little at a screen. Else escaping from such eye fatigue to be trapped with other people in a small room, meeting over something?

My guess is that there's a lot of slack and the slack increases with the headcount. Twenty percent? Thirty or more in your kingdom? How would you know or measure it? The nature of work must be called into question – once again, as in previous chapters. What needs to be done? How can it be un-drudged; and who must make the coffee while we, the Masters, contemplate tomorrow?

Slack is mostly squeezed-out by headcount culls. How can pointless tasks be discovered and vaporized when humans need to cling to them to justify employment? Days are filled with the A, B and C prioritized tasks of diminishing impact on outcome.

Find the slack of the waiting-for-an-answer; the nothing-to-do-right-now and the no-priorities busy-ness. You'll be doing everyone favours where your insight and authority can stamp out the person-to-person delays and the machine-to-person frustrations.

24.

IRRATIONAL SYSTEMS

We know, nay hope, that all systems should be rational. I've met a few that were, but like irrepressible children, many others can do with a little discipline. For illogical reasons the designs were probably drawn up by committee or by casting the lot. Almost all follow the path to the deep wormhole of despair.

In the age of the Compliance Nerd, you can safely bet that the Won't-Offend system will drag its Won't-Be-Effective half-brother down with it. Throwing a zealous gatekeeper into the mix will get you a Molotov cocktail*.

Try to book your unworking appliance in at an iStore, only to get told you don't have an appointment to be standing at the counter. Think about that for a moment – that requirement IS on the website, right? Not a chance. It's policy. It becomes a procedure. That's the System. Hell hath about the same fury as a consumer scorned. Can't produce your printed proof of purchase (they won't settle for the credit card slip)? Sorry. Cannot help you. And so on through demands for case numbers, and voila! – here's your System Chernobyl.

Go lose your innocence – use your own system as if you were a customer. You may well discover that it is a grumpy and unforgiving one that has needless options and unexplained time constraints. Don't be on a short fuse. How would *you* want to conclude the interaction, and how should you be shepherded? Get a Mystery Customer to crash your systems monthly.

Many on the inside who hold things back have a vested interest in keeping the status quo, while yours is to make your system a status symbol. Make it flow, open the blockages, up the standards,

---

* *Molotov cocktail is a home-made firebomb in a glass bottle, thrown by revolutionaries*

conquer the industry. Price and presentation may be great, but the phenomenal delivery of the promises made is the spark for the fireworks. "How do we do this? Why do we do that?" These are questions that pave the way to the pearly gates of Lasting Endeavours.

You want that throne. So don't tolerate irrational people, irrational decisions or irrational execution – don't settle for the irrational consequences of such systems.

25.

BETTER WEAPONS

Wars are fought with strategy and by troops, but better weapons can be decisive. In 1899 the Boer 7x57mm Mauser rifle didn't ballistically outperformed the British .303" Lee Enfield and Lee Metford– but having a smokeless propellant kept the shooter hidden, while the white-puffed British shot was exposed with absolute devastating consequences. The British clung to their outdated weapons into the 2nd Great War. Lunacy, but a telling illustration of the power of attachment to the familiar.

There you are, too. Clinging to your old weapons, brandishing DCF as a valuation when some unbearded youth whips out an operational free cashflow model as more accurate. You've been outshot. Ambushed by your intransience. His better weapon was crafted by his recent MBA or Financial Update Course – which you probably paid for but didn't heed. Lesson learned: update your armoury and keep it current.

Ditto your IT knowledge, where a Ponytail Man may calmly announce the choice of edge cloud computing as whupping your insistence on a cloud Disaster Recovery option. Selling? Ops? Even logistics have weapons to 'destruct your mass'. What about changes in CRM, the use of AI in disseminating Big Data and its integration into the sales cycle?

Listen and learn, ask and thrive – but know that even a polished sabre is no match for the musket, however well brandished by a competent but ageing arm. At least get the firebrand shooting on your command and not in your direction. New weapons bring new tactics, think *Bewegungkrieg* or 'blitzkrieg' war, that tanks and forward-thinking brought on against the Siegfried line. What are the possibilities, how far out of the box are the probabilities still worth the risk? Fight with the latest and fight with your smartest.

Test the new weapons, choose and master the better ones without nostalgia.

26.

Beware of ratchet-up

Gradualism is evil. A gesture can become a habit that becomes legacy, then heritage, onto tradition – and who knows where it will lurk to fang you in the gluteus? The year-end closing lunch first becomes a party with drinks. Next you need catering. Enter a 'dress-up' theme. Then wives are included. Then it must be with presents. Then they come to expect bonuses. Bussing of all is needed because of drunk-driving laws; then ubering them because of their varied destinations. Then it all crashes the budget.

Maybe you've been there or can remember the across-the-board 5% 'Christmas in July' salary hike. It's already June and everyone is getting nervous about the purchases already planned and you sense the icy silence seeping in under your closed office door. Many of these give-the-pinkie stunts are innocent when breezily offered once.

Beware of the creep – the push for an hour-earlier closings on Fridays – because of some good reason at the time. These are requests that feels offensive to boot out of the boardroom. Do you permit suckling moms at work? Allowing Twitter and Insta on corporate laptops 'just for lunchtime use'? Is there a pattern developing? Yes, it's human nature; water wears down the hardest rock. How about softer toilet paper, background music in reception, water coolers, McDonald's delivery, vending machines, car allowances – the perks will ratchet in only one direction, up – yours.

It will be seen as unfair when you start picking at the threads to unravel these privileges which have been transformed into rights. You had best be careful to avoid cultivating such a propensity in the first place. 'Employee comfort' is a Herzberg hygiene factor – hurtful when absent but not motivating by itself.

If you have to dismantle, take all of them down and then start afresh. Loosen the winches, unclick the ratchets. The names you will be called behind your back may expand your understanding of English – and some foreign languages too, but the test is whether all work-benefit from these concessions? And does everyone want to preserve these at the expense of bottom-line benefits?

27.

PEOPLE EXPAND INTO MONEY AVAILABLE

Laurence Peter's dictum of 'Work Expands into Time Available' is as true as it was in hippie-era 1969. The Unconventional CEO's dictum is that problems cannot be solved by bringing in more people but that management will still do its utmost to prove this wrong. Expanding? Add more people. There are problems or overworked departments that 'need more people'. Sales low? Add salespeople. If some salt improves the flavor, so let's keep adding more salt. You know where this is heading.

Staffing is that 'Swiss Knife' of resources: hugely productive at the sweet spot of efficiency and cost – but deadly where layered incompetence meet laid-back entitlement. In such constrained circumstances, get to the root of the evil and fix the structures, the processes, the activities and the controls. You need to keep the blades sharp.

Adding people means adding unguided complexity, which leads to unforeseen complications. Like adopting a child, it will mean you need some time to bed the situation down, and that may not be happening in a competitive environment with unpredictable adults. Your new hireling has a massive target on her back to her colleagues, is probably being paid more than the incumbents and is hell-bent on fixing their problems that they don't acknowledge or support.

Think the process of appointment through. Get colleagues' consent, get buy-in, involve the gatekeepers and settle the churning stomachs of those who feverishly hope that last-in, first-out will save their pensions if this disruption goes South.

Of course you pay them all less than they're worth; that's where the profit for the risk-taking comes from. Now that you are making a healthy margin, fixing the bits that are more grind than polish will require problem solving, not people adding.

28.

DO WE GET WHAT WE INCENTIVIZE?

Every dog hopes for that a reward after a trick and every circus owner knows that is the way it works – why are you hoping your team will 'self-incentivize' magically? It is a tad late to hope for the return of the '50's 'Company Man', who traded supreme loyalty for tenured security.

The semi-gig economists temporarily warming the seats are operating 60 years after the time when expectation of corporate allegiance came before personal beliefs. Is work a means to an end or a means to participate in the consumerism that credit-giving encourages?

In your own case, chances are that you served another company before this one and that you probably didn't marry your first sweet-heart. Offering incentives is a millennia-old method, and it is both an art and a science. Think beyong 'do this, get that reward'. The short answer is that explicitly stated, well understood, and satisfyingly accepted incentives do guide behaviour.

The circus is not only run with treats, the threat of the whip is also handy. The art is to know which to use and when, and the science is, of course, to calculate how much of each to bestow. What is the receptionist measured on, and what incentive should she be offered for extraordinary execution? The accountant? The storeman? The tea lady? Perhaps all of them.

Think Santa. Expect presents.

29.

THE LUXURY OF
UNINTERRUPTED TIME

Procrastination: thy name is Open Diary. Yes, the temptation to put Big Things off until a suitable Big Gap in the timeline is available is tempting – and often fatal. Proust could snuggle in for years while writing his novels in leisurely longhand but you, *compadre*, march to a more insistent and insanely-faster beat.

There's a CEO report wanted for incorporation into the Integrated Report, a MOU outline for your first foray into battery-powered widgets, an outline for succession planning, and so it continues on and on. What you may envisage as a close-my-door tranquility is a luxury.

That 05:00 wake-up before you hit the bike is your uninterrupted time, your solo slogging uphill with your sweat and thoughts are when you are on your own, able to think your own thoughts. This is where you lay the groundwork, foundations, fortifications and the other architecture of the 'long timeline' stuff. In reality you may have to do the report over several short sessions, and juggle it with a handful of other, getting-more-urgent, hot potatoes. Even writing your novel or *mémoires* is a stop-and-go project. *Carpe Diem!*

Relish those lesser minutes between the big moments of your day. You cannot afford to wait for the perfect shot at the perfect trophy specimen. It may or may not wander into your line of sight. Until then, it's a few short minutes to kick off and kick forward the things that will take hours to complete that may elude you in exquisite, luxurious and uninterrupted diary time slots.

Don't hesitate, wait or procrastinate. Push back against the tyranny of the clock and your own brief time on earth by making the moments count instead of counting them.

30.

STAYING ON AS THE CHIEF EXECUTIVE

Prussian war strategist Carl Von Clausewitz said that defense is easier than attack. Other war strategists Hart, Barnett, and even Sun Tzu alluded to the chances of a well-planned passive defense being able to repel an overwhelming attack. The job is yours to lose unless you chose it unwisely. Taking on a no-hoper, a nest of adders or a den of thieves, is a career-limiting choice.

Your ego must be subservient to your common sense – that's the premise of many of these pages. The excessive salary and perks, the emotional and enthusiastic interview or tour should raise red flags, if not your hackles. Some of our ilk die professionally in a blaze of fire and self-serving glory, but your spark must live on to fuel a deeper hue and longer glow in a steady furnace.

It is hard to brush-off the stardust from eager kingmakers, but you need to step up those stairs to the throne after staring up those same stairs objectively and dispassionately. Picking up that scepter means a commitment to holding and wielding it absolutely. Are you beholden to a tiresome Board or an attention-deficit founder? Better to find out first before the rituals for your crucifixion start.

The gods do favour a few of us, but Sophocles reminded us millennia ago that madness is a precursor to destruction by those same powers. Will that opportunity arise again if you let it slip away after doubting your powers to overcome? Only you can answer that, but will it be in glory or regret? The chances are good that your first shot at the top spot will be riskier than subsequent temptations. You're green, impressionable, hungry and what could go wrong?

Once in power, it's another universe. Everything in these three Unconventional books come into play, and there are much more conventional games too. Survival and growth of the enterprise –

and preserving your own place in it – is paramount. Enemies within are far more numerous and more dangerous than enemies without. Do you have weaknesses? Better overcome those snappy.

Make alliances, test for loyalty, affirm competence, generate dangerous enthusiasm, align for glory, execute against all odds, and scale the ramparts. Now you're safe for Year One. Weeding out the ill-fitting, re-arranging opportunities to match competencies and re-allocating priorities after your first victory lap should be easier but this is like waving the Jolly Roger* to the political assassination crowd and that's your skull on the flag.

Stay careful but determined – and delicate execution with great confidence will sustain you here; the streamlining has begun. Some enormously competent forces will oppose you; after all they would be next in line after your last mistake. Disloyalty is not a fireable offence but you, young Machiavelli, will have to set that exit up.

Remember only the Leader of the Pack breeds. Dissent drives creativity up to the point that the decision goes either with or against the unhappy and then a murmur becomes sedition with consequences. You cannot allow direct communication of your army with the politicians unless you sanctioned it, you can control it for time and content, and you are sure that the consequences are within your control. Anything else is back-stabbing.

However nice and wonderful you are going to come across, the line of command is the minefield that must not be overstepped by anyone; hierarchical organizations are formed and run like this for eons-old survival. Your Board looks to you for information and accountability. You blame no subordinates and none of them get the chance to blame you there. Offsite Board meetings are in order. Strict control and checks on access too.

Your defensive position must be clear and impregnable; as long as the Huns are kept out and the moola flows, you are the Man and only accolades are in order. Deviate from this and there's a carousel

---

* *Jolly Roger is the Pirates' skull & crossbones flag*

of assassins waiting to jump in to where performance was undercut by suspicion in the minds of selectively-informed higher-ups.

It is the two D's that Nature imposes: Dominate or enDure. Perform and command; your glory will be fermata**.

** *Fermata is the musical symbol for sustaining a note for a long time*

31.

PILPUL KILLS

The spillover from different religions to the uninitiated can have many unintended consequences. In some, the things taught in that religion (hard work and a keen awareness of time in Protestantism, a sense of community help in Catholicism) can give the practitioner a boost in competition against not-likeminded competitors.

Some attributes give the believer an advantage over the others in small ways. Traits form the people that practice these and it is astonishing to see which religions are becoming more accommodating to religious differences and also those which find moral differences reprehensible enough to invoke even death.

Teaching and demanding diversity and inclusiveness for some is a foolish one-sided disarmament in an unfair and unjust world. Certain less-deadly traits must be guarded against. Ever had a discussion with a lawyer that turned into a disagreement? In both trying to convince the other, you may find yourself verbally disadvantaged by an argument-trained opponent.

Pilpul is a Hebrew term for a kind of technical, nit-picking, evasive and micromanagement of the direction of an argument. It is a bit like argumentative ju-jitsu where the force of an argument is not refuted but used against itself. The principle of the argument is not opposed but waylaid by skillful and persistent death-by-a-thousand-cuts argumentation. "You were late again this morning". "What is late? I was at the gate – do I need to be at my desk? What about my leaving late yesterday, doesn't that show my loyalty? Is a minute that important or is my quality worth me staying? Why aren't the real slackers being punished? Could I please get that reserved parking spot I asked for to keep me from spending time finding parking space?"

That's argumentation. Pilpul is "what exactly is 'late' and who is measuring it with what calibrated timepiece – how 'late' was I?" It's the hair-splitting of minor and of major issues, it's the tying up in the Long Tails of argumentation instead of cutting to the chase. When does one have a 'beard'? Exactly how long must the whiskers be – one mm? Did anyone measure it? You get the point. Anything not This Morning Clean-Shaven is unshaven – the definition is not 'beard' but 'Clean Shaven'.

This clever pilpul-ling of issues is time-wasting, exasperating and reflects a poisonous state of mind. It's trying to be clever instead of owning up. It scores points instead of getting to a conclusion that needs half a word to be understood.

It is a slow undercutting by use of a malevolent attitude; it's a terrorist in your own midst. Every root and branch must be destroyed. Actions in rational order are what you want and must have, not doubters in opposition.

32.

Life changing "no"

Chose the cards you are holding? No, life dealt them without fear, favour or reason, not by your choice. You got the big ears and the impatience to match. The good looks fell to the school stud. Cleverness was bestowed to others and bodily ability was dealt in spades to some of the most undeserving fellas. Those cards didn't look too promising.

Pick up and play. Expect to win. Expect the timing to be rotten, outside of your control and perfectly unpredictable. That's the good news. The bad news is that access to the playing table is impeded by plentiful of sharp elbows, stomping feet and a thunderous cascade of that world you have to conquer in order to lay your claim, build your dream and rule your empire: the NO.

This is the closed door, the bolted gate and the forbidden shortcut. Overcoming NO is your mission, your test and your key to the wonderland beyond. NO means 'this is not your path'. NO means: not now, not this, not this way. In essence, if NO is the answer, you were not meant to ask that question; you are meant to Hannibal-in-the-Alps it: *aut inveniam, aut faciam* – either find a way or make one.

You have to do this on your own, in your way and at your own cost. NO is the most painfully liberating word – it cuts you from the dependence or another's YES that you cannot control. You now have to be in charge of getting what you want without asking. You wanted it, now go get it.

Once found, your life is transformed from dependence to mastery. It may take a while to grow the muscles needed to pull your chariot and expect a few stumbles on the way – but you are off your knees and eye-to-eye with the competition. Make rivals of your idols. Thank the naysayers; they put up the hurdle that tested you and made you unleash your spirit of can-do.

33.

What are you dressing up?

If Ferrari launched a premium champagne brand would it succeed? Would you pay more for good champagne because of the name on the label? What does 'Ferrari' add to the taste? Perhaps deep inside, the bloke with that bottle in hand is contemplating that he's over-paying for the champagne – as surely as the Ferrari name added to the price. Ferrari added nothing to the value.

Perhaps it was the perception, perhaps the allure or some convoluted status thing. However, Ferrari wasn't offering Dom Perignon at a better price under Ferrari label. Now if you import or assemble or resell a brand and add your margin on top – what value are you actually adding?

You may be dressing up something at a value point to its detriment – unless you can dress it down to a better price point. 'Odd Bins' works as a wine concept. So do house brands. Distributing HP's products at their widely recommended price point makes purchase sense. The value is known, the elasticity of the price in a market is tested. Getting more margin would mean that more value needs to be added – more volume of ink in the cannister, trade-in on the cannister or free software upgrades when purchasing in bulk or something the printer owner would appreciate.

Dressing up to your brand – unless you add something special – is as sustainable as a tire with a slow puncture. The Ferrari brand champagne is selling for less than half the price of Moët. What does that do to the Ferrari brand?

At one stage, South Africa had 26 cellular distributors. All me-too and nothing extra; same price and same phones. None survived their complications, all dressed up and prancing they fell to competition. None dressed-down in cost savings, none added value.

Good night and good luck, boys. Hard lessons were learned.

34.

'MESEARCH'

As opposed to research, mesearch is continuous, loosely focused, mostly unscientific and self-assembling; adding information to the mix and then finding patterns and insight. Mesearch is the gears grinding away in your head while your eyes are open, and also often when they flutter in REM* behind tired lids.

Mesearch is also the focused hoovering-up of info, data, trends, failures and gossip. And then comes the testing, trying, applying, rejecting, formulating and repeating, both in the width of as well as in the depth of the insight, hoping something useful may stick to the neurons.

Mesearch can blindside you if you keep following only the easy trail and waste your efforts. Your feelers should yearn to touch and explore the areas that you are not well informed in, that elude your understanding or that just doesn't make sense to your world, like the Bitcoin thing. Or how Musk survives and prospers. Even why the 100-year virus cycle repeats.

Hunting consists mainly of wandering in unknown terrain and being hyper-attentive to what you want to find. Mesearch likewise is looking for clues that help or hinder, learning along the way to freshen your camo kit and keep you abreast of what may or may not influence you.

Mesearch is listening to many and varied voices; it is personal. It clogs and then may alter your filters but mesearch is your business radar. You want to talk to the competition and their clients, search for new slants on finding future prospects and endlessly scroll though the curious websites you bookmarked through the years in preference to the mainstream narratives. Such insights could gain

---

* *Rapid Eye Movement is the dream state of sleep*

you a couple of race centimeters or a month ahead of the soon-to-be has-beens in your industry.

These informative breaks are yours to find, deploy and enjoy. Mesearch is your prowling subconscious with a deadly intent: find the prey before others do.

35.

RUN THE BUSINESS NOT THE NUMBERS

Kenny Rogers sang it best in The Gambler:

> *You've got to know when to hold 'em*
> *know when to fold 'em*
> *Know when to walk away know when to run.*
> *You never count your money*
> *while you're sittin' at the table*
> *There'll be time enough for countin'*
> *When the dealin's done.*

How do you apply Don Schlitz"s song's approach to common sense business strategy? What is it to run the business, not the numbers? What is Kenny's gambler's lesson? The numbers are a guide that sets the way towards *Shambhala*.

This mythical place, of which Three Dog Night sang so well, lives in the fables as that place where the mountains cleave and a passage wide enough for only one man to traverse opens into paradise. It does so only once in a lifetime. Miss it and your dream dies. Is your focus on careful steps on the narrow mountain path in front of you (the numbers) or on the peaks on the horizon (the business)?

Climbing the Rupina La pass is a daunting Nepal Himalaya journey and it is advisable to watch your every step. Concentrating only on your progress means you'll see only the next 5 meters of mountain path and little else. It is safe but the meaning and magnificence of the trip is lost.

There are parts that need climbing with rigid attention – but it matters more to focus on where you're heading and what the breathtaking scenery on the journey is like. You don't walk for weeks to get tired or for distance, you walk for the exhilaration of the journey.

The paths must be watched and followed as the money rolls in. The cause of richness is the business of travelling and not the steps taken.

Lift your eyes and your spirit will follow.

36.

How good is Personal Attention?

Some obsess over their businesses. Not surprisingly these obsessives also tend to succeed. It is not the only path to success but when the owner of Pretoria's upmarket Cream restaurant personally inspected every plate that was served up during the first five years of operation, he succeeded. Then there was a chance that standards might waiver a tad when he took his first vacation.

Didn't the staff get the message all these years of the perfect serving? Hadn't they been exposed to scorching OCD insistence? How could they not know what to deliver? In delegating that ruby laser focus, know that there's no-one like you. A one percent deviation, unchecked, can land a pilot in another country after some hours of flying time. No, staff are not you, and never will be.

What is a reasonable expectation when handing over the reins by delegation? Ask for clarification of your set standards. Ask how the task is understood. Ask 'how will this be performed?' Ask how it will be managed, if kept on track and in check. Then listen (as outlined in the next chapter). There's your answer.

People are who they are. They will revert to doing the things they usually do. Expecting a difference is a little … naive? Stupid perhaps? At least get consensus on the goals and how these will be measured. Let them find their own inner temporary superhero – but watch the results. It is their personal attention that will ensure results.

Nature abhors a vacuum; the absence of presence will lead to the presence of interpretation – doing things that are comfortable instead of uncomfortably correct. Personal attention is a resetting compass, a verification of correctness and a confirmation of competence.

It is your spirit that imbues the weary but only when it is close to the hands that labour.

37.

HOW TO LISTEN

Listen to understand, not to answer. Men generally listen in order to propose a solution. Women generally listen with empathy. How can your ears work better? Chew the tongue, clench the teeth or just furrow the botoxed areas somewhat. Do listen, though. To listen deeply first and then darting a reply is like a slow-motion knock-out punch instead of death by a thousand verbal jabs. In Pirsig's book 'Lila', he described the Cheyenne culture; a man attending a tribal elder meeting, as

> Slow to speak, eager to listen, describing himself as a person of no-importance, humbly presenting his points carefully in a way that is overwhelming and decisive.

This is a good personal strategy. Being underrated is an advantage. Obtaining extra information to strengthen your argument is good positioning. Keep asking questions and listen intently until you know how the other side's mind is made up. Make it your gift to come across as being understanding.

To prompt good listening, good questions are required from you. This art must reside in your quiver of attack weaponry. Perfect practice makes perfect. Pose the open-ended question for information and the closed ended question to confirm you have grasped it.

Take time to formulate your reply in response to the new information. Confirm with them what you heard them say. Lay out its implications. Show the good points and then the flaws. Agree on the good points then obliterate the flaws with clear logic. Describe how the outcomes can be enhanced. Ask for their support as it is a 'joint outcome': their good points and yours. Listen to their responses and signs of acceptance or not. You were told and you listened and now you are the custodian of that information and those arguments.

Keep it professional and resist the easy personal targets. Live up to your Solomonic reputation.

Once all is understood, your reply should be sage and decisive without you needing to stick the eagle feathers in your man bun as a show of victory.

38.

Passing of time

Mono no aware is a touch of Japanese nostalgia. In loose translation, it is the acute awareness of the passing of time. Time and tide wait for no man. In its deepest essence you, now at the height of your powers as a CEO, must accomplish the duality of living in the glorious moment of straddling a part of the universe, while staying off the Ozymandias* track of FIGJAM**. You are creating the future while planning to exit it sometime too.

That's how life is; a wonderful crested wave that will end in froth on a rocky shore, never to be repeated. What a sad species we are to live only once, be so acutely aware of it and then deny it's temporariness so vociferously.

Moaning about *mono* will pass the time a wee bit faster – a double dose of loss as time wasted and time passed. Being and staying so aware of the endless ticking while you surf, hunkered down in the barrel on you 'log is moment after moment of fleeting ecstasy, just to end into the nothingness of the past that you can only relive in vivid recall but never repeat.

The moment is yours; the juice of life and the power of your accomplishments is now. Then it passes; imperceptibly slowly but relentlessly through the 2,6 million seconds every month. Each one ready for the taking; and lost a moment later. You have this empire to rule – an empire of fleeting time and choices. As Harrison Ford's character Dr. Jones was told by the last Keeper of the Grail when viewing the several possible goblets: 'Choose wisely'.

---

* *Ozymandias was an Egyptian Pharaoh who boasted his unforgettable might inscribed on a colossus. Alas he and his ruins are forgotten by history.*

** *Fck I'm Great Just Ask Me*

39.

DUKKHA

There is wisdom in the belief that an inner stillness can help straighten a hectic life. This stillness is not an emptiness but an ordering of the chaos between urgent and the important; between useful thoughts and pure distraction and indulgence. Such stillness is hard to obtain and even more difficult to maintain. Life is ticking past, faint voices of future victories cry out for attention.

Dukkha is an eastern concept that is worth understanding. It is the creeping irritation of impending and inevitable change. Perhaps you now have dukkha in relation to your money pile quest, whilst someone somewhere is chasing blondes on his yacht and planning for his kids to increase his stash. It is the feeling when some Young Turks really do bring home more bacon than anyone has seen in a while. It's knowing that you, a fellow CEO, have a sell-by date.

It's *dukkha* that irritates to the points of distraction into substance abuse. It's not taming a desire but satisfying a persistent nagging that leads to an addiction. Dukkha cannot be ignored; you must acknowledge it and manage it in the knowledge that change is inevitable. Your permission is not always sought when the world transitions.

Can you steer towards better outcomes for yourself without dukkha on your shoulder? Can you master maturity to the point of accepting inevitable demise even before you summon up the energy to start the task? Everything temporary is dukkha, even happiness. It will change. So will you.

In your quest for more and better, do not let the dukkha keep you back or dissuade you from achieving what you set out to so fearlessly once.

40.

THE HEDONISTIC TREADMILL

Roman slaves were generally worked very hard, treated as chattel and identified by short-cut hair, tattoos and restricted to a single wife, if any at all. The elite wallowed in luxury and delight, sporting long tresses, fair skin and multiple-liaisoned lifestyles of no hard work.

Which are you? Some of us are guilt-ridden Protestants acting like the slaves of yore. Hard work, one wife, all in for a better future for the kids. This is the narrow and rocky road. It is amassing wisdom and riches in a never-ending toil of improvement and service.

Others have lives like those elites, luxuriating and lording over minions.

You see the hedonistic treadmill daily; it may repel you in disgust or attract your envy. Are you part of the club or a stern critic? Should people be allowed to spend their money on the overpriced trivia of life? Or spend other people's tax money as pampered *apparatchiks*?

The question above leads to the following exercise in executive soul-searching: How much hedonism is too much, if any is even allowed? It's zero if the company has to pay. Nil, nada and nothing. It must be financed in the same way charity is funded: it comes from your own pocket. Do you order that bottle of sought-after Trapiche Malbec at a lunch with clients and justify it to accounts?

Make it easy on yourself and on everyone that orbits you: indulgences are personal expenses. These include alcohol and tips. That includes the X6 rental where you could have settled for the Corolla. Or business class when you're not stepping off the plane and right into a meeting, in which case you would have been saving a night's accommodation. The Mont Blanc purchased on a corporate credit card?

Here is the principle: if it's your money, spend it yourself from your *salarium* or dividends. If it's the shareholders' money, be like the Good Servant and multiply it. Corporate hedonism is a cancer and you must wring its neck early.

Your own proclivity to the Good Life is another choice entirely. What's questionable here is probably why you tend to run to indulgence – were you brought up that way or is it an attempt to compensate for a meagre youth? Slave or Master? Builder or Enjoyer?

If your inner fire is all-consuming, when do you flip the role from slave to master, if at all? Apologies if you are slightly uncomfortable with this question. It is pertinent in a world where, not so long ago, the sign of a rich man was that he did not need to work. It is a larger and richer world now thanks to billions of hands toiling uncountable hours daily in search of a dream of betterment in a consumption-led economy.

The kicks to be had are legion; some man-caves bristle with endorphin pumping toys and some waistlines are testaments to good living. Perhaps you can sample the poison from time to time but stay the master thereof – it should be an adventure and not a treadmill.

This is only my opinion. Catholic of Hedonist? The Now or the Hereafter? Perhaps age and maturity matter where bling becomes patina; the oldies tend to opt for the classics of simple but good taste; heed again the words in Hamlet, the advice by father Polonius to Laertes the student son:

> *Costly thy habit as thy purse can buy,*
> *But not express'd in fancy; rich, not gaudy;*
> *For the apparel oft proclaims the man…*

As for living the good life, temptations abound. What is moderation? What is enough? Decide for yourself and stick to simple rules. Never impress. Never waste. Never bite off more than what can be chewed with ease and satisfaction.

41.

Opposing views

To be moved, people want to be persuaded, not merely informed. Your casual 2 cents worth is seldom seen as sage footnotes of information if it challenges a firmly held opinion. Opposing stances are taken personally by most of your fellow bipeds. A detracting comment, correction or snippet is not appreciated unless asked for. It is as if ideas are welded to the character of the person, no-one is allowed to play the devil's advocate anymore. Why pull a knife if you're not looking for a fight?

Words denote dominance struggles, views and argument-wins indicate clever genes to the opposing sex, and a misfire here could lead to your DNA being cast on the scrapheap if you're not careful in your tidbits. If you oppose a view, go gently but

...Beware
Of entrance to a quarrel; but being in,
Bear't that th' opposed may beware of thee.
Give every man thine ear, but few thy voice

Advice again from old and wise Polonius. Listen, clarify and then set out to persuade, not to argue or counter-inform. Trading barbs for fun is tiring to both sides and unresolved issues can fester. Take up the challenge if you must. Don't argue to entertain or just to hear your own melodious voice reverberating.

Many will just clam-up on hearing your counter proposal – due to your status, perhaps time constraints or the close availability of a heavy object that can be swung in a short deadly arc towards your head. Persuasion must end in their buy-in, acceptance, change of position and the admission of the newly set standard. Argue the facts, the wisdom, the improved outcome which this will lead to, as well as the objectivity of your stance. It should not be just *your* argument' but a gentle pointing out that there were hidden truths to be uncovered.

If you need some ammunition for a war of attrition, in the 'Rulebook for Arguments', author Anthony Weston advises on how to undo an argumentative charlatan's tricks. Crap is spoken as a second language by many, but rather avoid and dismiss this – unless you have no other hobbies or loved ones wanting to take you home soon and in good spirits.

As for suffering fools, to gently change the subject to something more trivial instead of drawing lines in the sand, is a wise option. Those who cannot take criticism is best cut from future conversations.

42.

THE 97% RULE

'The **bane** of your existence' – the Viking term refers to poison. Exactly how many things in your professional and home life are almost done…. but which are waiting for a final something to reach completion? Almost there … but not quite, can be your bane.

Let's call it 97% done, but all in limbo. The reasons and explanations for this can fill books, but in the real world such progress means little – the 97% is wasted time, effort, money, emotions – until the final piece of the jigsaw magically fits into place. Serious money bets that you are very familiar with this situation and that the intestinal bacterium *Helicobacter Pylori* gnaws the stomach-lining into ulcers whenever you view the list of the 'Tasks (Almost) Done'.

You are not alone, but you're part of a giant and pathetic army of mortals down in Dante's First Circle of Hell – Limbo. Sadly you will be drawn down to Circle Five (wrath); perhaps via a quick sideroad of Frustration to Seven (Violence) and into Despair, which is your own 10th circle.

Your salvation lies in keeping this list short and on-the-trot. Boxes must be ticked and new issues are birthed, seemingly to test you. Demand lists from your people – but monitor their progress and lead them out of the sin of 'I-was-waiting-for…'

For this, there is, unfortunately, no Dantian forgiveness.

43.

THE SECOND BOYFRIEND

In Argentina there's a joke about the frustration of the first boy-friend of a chaste and good girl. They laughingly declare it's the second boyfriend that gets the spoils – to the dismay of the well-behaved first one.

The lesson is that both boys got what they expected. It is a crude way to describe life and not every girlfriend/boyfriend is recently escaped from the nunnery. Perhaps you are not the first every time, perhaps never? What are your expectations of the next project you tackle – will it echo the success of the first boyfriend or the second?

Crank-up your expectations and live a little. Business is there for the taking, grab it with double hands-full and don't look back. Look at the timidity amongst your own Lifers – what would it take to get them salivating to score big? Your permission to chase down their dreams and goals? Encourage them to lift their eyes a bit higher, to reach out toward further horizons. Some may wilt, but most should prosper.

When shy girls take off their glasses the world becomes a better place, and so should all the magnificent but restrained talent that files in at 08:00 sharp.

Rise up, conquer and live a meaningful life with deep memories!

44.

APOPHENIA

It's useful to know how minds work. Perhaps it's critical to at least know your own foibles. A number of majestic books describe the complete idiocy of man using a cranial tool that overshot the evolutionary trajectory by a logarithmic number.

If you want smarts, wisdom and a superbly predictable behavior, consider the honeybee with only 25,000 neurons. Remarkable. Irrationality in contrast, comes in a 2 kg jelly-like mass of Omega 3 lipids nestled between human ears zinging along a few trillion synapses.

It is rather difficult to believe that we're the Lord's finest creation– perhaps His prototype but, then again, the Neanderthal had 15% more brain size than us. Is there a trajectory of use-it or lose-it?

When the mind makes arbitrary connections between unlinked things it's either Picasso and Tesla or Joe Sixpack on conspiracy theories. We absolutely crave completion to our thoughts and will make up links and postulate why things are what we think they are. Facts are often correctly shown to be related, but the complexities of life create an enormous amount of possibilities – and cutting through this jungle is hard enough without these connections made.

We live in this *Apophenia*, where we see order and patterns in quite random events and images. We make sense for ourselves even to our detriment. We do not wait for the full picture; we jump to conclusions; we in-fill as a general shortcut to the biases we have and fight logic and truth. Luckily this behaviour is so common that we expect it and are forgiven for changing our minds rapidly and often – even embarrassingly so. The world must fit our reality, we are correct and reality must adapt to us.

Your reputation as a sage is one wrong assumption and conclusion away from a career-damaging dent. No one should remind you to better check the veracity of their assumptions, and of course you have to check your own, too. It's Darwin again: variety of possible connection, check!; choice of the verified correct, check! Repeat.

You must conquer apophenia, it could be *apoplexia* if you lose.

45.

REGRESSION TO THE MEAN

Clever traders swear by old truths. Whenever a commodity price blows out or collapses (oil may be at $20 today, but this will probably never be repeated), they shrug and say that it is temporary and will settle at its long-term average price. Super profits attract competition or alternatives.

In a reasonably free market everything becomes affordable or goes bust. The eternal search will go on for an angle, a unique selling point, and advantages that cannot be copied. The search is never ending and you will have to make hay in the sunshine of your delight but keep moving.

Telecoms went from super-margins to just marginal. Diamonds are now synthetic. Multi-valve engineering excellence evolved to the Tesla 13-moving-part electric drivetrain that threatens the fuel engine. Timing is critical. There are gaps between reality and the Regression to The Mean and time's a-wasting.

Marx's 'Crisis Theory' laughed at capitalism's falling profits in a competitive world. So did J.S. Mill and famed David Ricardo in their penmanship. Those economists proclaimed a warning to be heeded; adapt or die, improve or perish, get better or else you will get lost in the rush to the place where you found your gold.

It's Schumpeter's *Creative Destruction* and Christensen's *Innovator's Dilemma*; these may have crossed your desk at study time just to show regression to the mean is not a new or a fringe issue. Sharpen up!

46.

BIG DISASTERS

You steady your hand. The dice fly. It has been a long time coming and you have a compelling vision of the future. The Board bought into it. The pitch was for serious funds, the outcomes were going to be Next Level stuff. The timing is perfect and the buzz is invigorating. All are holding their breath as the cubes clatter to a marvelous outcome. Not.

It's Snake-Eyes. Double Ones. Game over.

Henry Ford threw badly – not once, but twice. Fordlandia was to be the conquering of South American jungle for the propagation and delivering of natural rubber. All came to naught and Ford still owns 150,000 unplanted Brazilian hectares. It had been a brilliant idea and is still worth reading about. Then Henry decided to stop the Model T production before the Model A was ready. It took two years and while cars were produced. The logic here was convoluted. Ford never regained its lost place as the world's foremost automaker. Double the deuce.

What prompts such enormous disasters? Think Boeing, Sasol, Time-Warner – in fact about a third of all listed companies disappear every decade. Small oopsies can hurt but a corporate Armageddon is spectacular in its wealth-destruction avalanche. Mergers from Hell (also a book), details sound decisions that were overtaken by unforeseen events and plain goddamn stupidity of the Olympic kind.

Betting the farm is a dicey move at all times. Catching up on the promised 10% growth via a Big Leap acquisition can pull the sinews off the bone – and often does. More than half of world-wide public mergers and acquisitions are disappointments. Out of the hundreds of daily decisions you will make from your super ergonomic chair, a momentary lapse of reason can undo your vision and the cacophony of crashing value may deafen you permanently.

No one plans for a Black Hole event but the proverbial stuff can hit fans with monotonous regularity. Hot Shots with credentials far exceeding yours have made history-altering bloopers. How should you inoculate against this?

47.

BIG DISASTERS – *CONTINUED*

The best advice in dealing with most disasters is not to cause them in the first place. That's an oxymoron, true, but the final decisions in risky moves should be taken by those with the most to lose – owners.

The conservative in you may be tempted out of your shell towards the limelight – a moth to a flame or an upcoming star to the Oscar podium – if this idea of yours comes to fruition. Those are the extremes, and the heartbeat in your throat should be your guide.

The Pareto of disaster avoidance are 'Big Steps' and 'Short Cuts'. Big Steps will mean neglecting current business to focus on the exciting new and expansive task. Big Steps means a threat of school fees and new experiences to come of unforeseen snags, timing issues and the inevitable over-cost and under-income curve before the fireworks start dazzling the world.

Can you afford it – company wise and career wise? The fruit of your industry is generally late. Much of this book, and of my previous tomes are rah-rahs into breaking, conquering and building. The caveat is always there: if the buffalo is wounded it will turn on you with a vengeance. From trophy to tomb, from valedictory to funerary oration in seconds. You had better aim well and shoot straight. Contingencies? Back-up Professional Hunter with a falling-block big bore rifle? Take smaller steps, form coalitions, perform dry-runs, secure insurance and undertake risk management before that stratospheric leap where risks exposes the shareholders.

"Short Cuts' are tempting. Walking a tightrope between genuine process savings and cheap shortcuts asks for a great deal of common sense, the type that can evaluate the consequences of a move gone wrong. Can it be easily rolled-back? If yes then go install the automated Amazon pickers instead of overworked staff. Mission critical in a hiccup? If yes then don't farm out the Boeing 737 MAX software to Indian part-timer coders.

Be bold but careful; change the world imperceptibly. Own up if the wobbles start – the greater the goal the more-wise guys should be on your team and they all are already on the payroll, tasked to solve problems. Make them earn it.

48.

CRISIS

Let's define a crisis as an unforeseen threat as well as being new, unknown and dire. It is not yet a disaster. You may end in deep negative territory with your business. It is the drop-everything alert to ensure survival.

Crises have unreasonable time-constraints. The usual management 'W's of What, Where and When changes to a 'T's' of That, There and Then. The 'Why?' of the crisis can be dealt with when the dust has settled. Your crisis experiences will mostly revolve around the immediate lack of cash – due to whatever issue Black Swanned you. Fire, flood, theft of IP, competitive maneuvers, the departure of personnel – all have an impact on the Lubricant of Business.

Lack of funds are the symptoms and has to be dealt with to save the patient. The consequences can be felt and dealt with tomorrow, but when the needle is in the red on the bank dashboard it signals CRISIS in a terrifying way. A sudden downgrade of the bonds in your rainy-day kitty, a bank clampdown on your credit, debtor claiming *vis major*; let me count the ways that crisis can entrap the unwary.

However you define it, the cost of the crisis will be in cash. How deep will you delve or how wide will you seek the solutions to a crisis is the unknown – and you would have spent a whole career in stocking the toolbox with hopefully enough preventative measures, plus a number of killer apps, to circumvent the fallout.

Have you anticipated it – and just in case it's is a genuine sucker punch – have you salted away the reserves to ride it out to the point of fixing the cause?

Expect the best – prepare for the worst; it's a nasty jungle out there.

49.

PULLING UP OR PULLING DOWN

Gravity can be your friend – if you're a golfer. It's easier down than up and it may shape your response to the minions when blame is on the menu. It is easier to pull people down to a level where shouting and vituperative spitting can ease the death grip around your angry ticker.

It is far more difficult to pull them up to your level where they must accept their responsibility of what caused your annoyance – and then for them to fix it. It is time-consuming and even tiresome to do the analysis of what went wrong and why. It is and remains necessary to guide and get understanding of future preventative actions in the perpetrator's mind.

You are the professional who brings meaning to imperfect people's work aspirations. Mistakes, misjudgments and myopia need to be corrected and a number of other oversights, too. Stupidity and negligence beg for discipline. Purposeful mistakes are unforgivable and, as noted before, they ensure the fastest ticket to an unemployment line without a company reference letter to help.

If blowing your top is your shortcut to save time and energy, you are certainly a temporary chair-warmer in the corner office. There are legendary hot-tempered business icons, but as an Unconventional you can imagine just how much better they could have been without a scared, resentful or outright-hostile crowd of associates.

It is harder to nurse a tree than to chop it down – but there's a life-long reputation of excellence ahead of you that will attract like-minded enthusiasts who would like to learn and grow in your shadow without the fear of you pushing the flame-thrower button. Your behaviour sets the tone, and this cascades down. Being the A**hole generates a company full of clones.

That's never you.

50.

WHAT WOULD YOU DO IF YOU HAD BETTER PEOPLE?

This little game of expectation can yield some surprising answers. It is just a nudge to loosen your grip on your reins.

What if ?

This can be played in many of your dark corners. What if you could cut out the middleman? What if you could charge more? An effective unmasker is the 'what if we had better people' postulate. It should give you some perspective on who you think needs replacing, who isn't up to the challenge, and which of the captains are on top of their game.

'What if?' jolts the subconscious and you should instinctively provide an answer before the social filters kick-in and all deficiencies can be explained. What if we had a better CEO? Who are the obstacles in the way of reaching our present needs?

Are there too many or too few in the command structure or the trenches? What thing would we be able to be if we could only find someone to do it or to lead the way?

The sobering after-party questions are crucial; you must do the best you can with who you have – or you should find better people if you cannot nurture a better person out of each of them.

51.

DECOMPOSING PROBLEMS

The knotted brow of frustrated subordinates presents itself daily in many guises. If the mission was easy to solve, anyone could have done it. Your ability to skillfully cut through the essence of problems and effortlessly steer around the rocks and shoals of a troubled sea is reflected in your generous remuneration, Alexander.

The heart of problem solving is decomposing problems and not fermenting them into nastiness. It's Father Time constraining you again. Speedy execution is preceded by speed of finding THE solution to an unexpected issue. Your deep understanding of such problems, complemented by your wide circle of fellows, should wrestle that recalcitrant animal to the ground and hog-tie it for steaks.

Procrastinated problems ferment from Important to Urgent and then escalate to Overwhelming in their own surprising time. Not every problem has the luxury of Fabius Maximus'*15-year delay of an Italian battle with the invader Hannibal. Quarterly results are due and there's an item on the Agenda under 'Outstanding' that burns your cheeks.

Problem-solving is a teachable skill with a logical structure; this approach should be to get to the real cause of the crisis first. More often than not, it generates a number of answers that should each be tested and evaluated before a final committed choice is made.

In a digital world the microsecond solution is expected. The analogue approach of dissect, think, ponder and choose may seem more like slow decomposition but it's the proper method to tick-off the worrisome items. Problems arise at every level of organization and it's perhaps your best legacy to standardise a method to detect and destroy the threats.

---

* *Fabius Maximus was the Roman Emperor who finally defeated Hannibal the Carthaginian*

Decomposing is active, fermentation is procrastinated time. The only good that fermentation generates is the sound to reward winners with popping Champagne corks.

52.

The swings of dominance

The most interesting aspect of cricket is the way the players experience changes in their fortunes. Batsmen have 'a run of luck' or a 'purple patch' and then it's back to the humiliation of a pair*. There are swings of in-form and then useless roundabouts of performances at the crease.

Bowlers, too, get in the groove for a while and then they can't seem to hit a barn door with an inswinger. At least the fielders are fairly stable, and mistakes are so uncommon that howlers are replayed on the TV to everlasting embarrassment.

Are you an opening bat or a slip fielder? Are you subject to periods of a golden touch, followed by leaden hands? The difference is that in the more menial tasks like fielding, the expectations for your 100% record is high. In the hallowed moments of facing the speeding ball as a batsman, things are less predictable, and the stakes are as high as the tension.

There will be times when you perform at your peak. Soon the wheels of fortune may favour others. It is a temporary situation of setback, but only if you see and approach it that way. When things don't swing your way you need to hunker down, admit the situation and spread the decision-making around for a while until your mojo comes back.

Roll with the punches, assess the circumstances; is it mildly disruptive or Death-Star-approaching urgent? Is it your sloppy thinking or have you experienced another personal trait of inattention? A little introspection in answering these questions must lead you back to improved self-confidence.

---

* *A pair is the colloquial for scoring two ducks (no runs) in successive innings of a cricket game*

Cricket teams tend to tumble when their captain fails; know that your self-doubt will be contagious – so stop it! You can't be perfect, at least not all of the time, but your teammates expect the world from you. Get your rhythm back as soon as feasible; but refrain from tackling biggies in your downswing cycle.

53.

CONSENSUS

This is a dangerous word.

The concept of 'consensus' must be understood and used carefully. It is the antithesis of a power structure. It is pliable, comforting and regularly regrettable. At its best, consensus is the agreed outcome when alternatives and misgivings have been settled to a point where it's an all-in, and the consequences will be borne equally.

At worst, it is the catching of a falling knife which had been dropped with bad intentions. Consensus could be a front for the passive-aggressive and the timid. It could be the 97% game of almost-there but nowhere done. It is a game of power and politics and of personal outcomes versus group dynamics. It is a tricky objective that must slowly and carefully be calmed and subdued.

Demanding consensus may invoke apathy and withdrawal of support. Active consensus is the commitment of the group with integrity, personal respect and trust. Consensus must be built in steps of agreement without ending in the humorous cliché of a camel-designed-by-committee. The 'asking' instead of 'telling' approach is a good start if you want to walk the consensus road. It requires small steps of selling your vision to hardened professional nay-sayers.

Between two people it is merely seen as reaching 'agreement'. The real consensus challenge involves aggregating a similar agreement, without much change or difference amongst more participants. The more people and the more complex the task, the steeper the slope becomes. You will hope for a smooth trajectory.

When the news of a massed Soviet Army on the Eastern Front is suddenly thrust upon you, time becomes a luxury and consensus may evaporate in favour of a rapid response. The dynamics change and those who felt their advice was once heeded on the high altar of consensual decisions may not be able to gear down professionally.

The vehicle skids; you are behind the wheel. To solely decide and then to persuade all on implementing what you alone have resolved has become difficult in an instant. At times, it does look as if corporate dictatorship has its advantages.

Follow your instincts. In peacetime, it may be easier to let your positional power flow down – as long as it is clearly understood that as the *Geshätsführer** you sometimes need to have the final – and sometimes the only – say.

---

* *Geshätsführer is Business Manager*

54.

GIBEs

A *gibe* is to utter a taunting word, to deride or tease with what you say; it's common among boxers. Would you stand for that? Would you stand for a worse type of GIBE: Good Idea, Badly Implemented? This should taunt you and deride you – if you are vulnerable to a gibe.

Let's start with your level of expectation for the job: Olympian, National or Regional? What level will you be expecting in terms of quality and timing? Did you set this out up-front, and were you clear on what will constitute success? Did the team accept this, buy into the parameters and pledge their commitment to Gold? Silver? or just a participation medal?

Architects, builders and engineers get away with the dreaded VO – the Variation Order. It's a professional shrug of 'not-my-fault' that will be reflected on the client's bottom line – and negatively so. You should be clear on the permitted variations and timing issues, and even offer a juicy bonus for completion ahead of D-Day.

Reputations will be enhanced. Fortunately, the weak links will also be exposed, and the CEO should carefully observe the interactions in both good and bad spells of chasing-down the prize. Reward and punishment should be on the menu, and you must include yourself, too.

Let's assume you've navigated this run of Deliverance. Excellent. In your periphery you may notice that everything visible around you was an idea once – and that not all history was artic lights of surreal luminescence. It went from idea to reality in Good Idea, Great Implementation.

Don't ever settle for a GIBE. As part of your path of never-ending improvement, set the standard and when necessary, redo the horrible and dysfunctional with enthusiastic rewards. Let none dare gibe you, champ.

55.

ON GETTING FIRED

Been there; done that – and you may sing the same hymn too. This is not an easy bite to 'Eat it Up' as Frank Sinatra sang in "My Way". I fired myself once – that witches' den of a corporate contraption imploded from incompetence soon thereafter. It was time for *schadefreude** – I knew I had to be on MY way and settling for less than what I thought I could achieve was never going to bring inner rewards.

Your Way often abides by the old adage that any stick will do if you want to beat a dog. The Board makes up its mind – often short-sightedly – that somewhere between Performance and Fit there's a gap that needs to be filled and it's not a task for you. Don't fight it; like a bad romance, she made up her mind a while ago and was looking for an excuse. Time to go with dignity.

It's difficult on the ego, but easier on the character; you are the same model that strutted in on Day One – just wiser and wilier. It is time to take stock and get through the four-or-so phases of grief in record time. It's not personal, it's professional, even if it felt a tad like knives being twisted. Forget searching for the reasons, the Stoic in you sees it clearly: it is what it is.

The biggest self-realignment is for your future direction. If you feel you failed in performance, put out your CV as surely you only failed in the end and have a World Cup contender track-record. If you feel betrayed in the corporate world's enslavement of your talent, there is tough love ahead; it's time to stake out your own patch and hang out your new shingle stating MINE.

You are the overperformer that ripped the hidden jealousies from the pathetic and the weak; the slave driver that ran the place

---

* *Schadefreude is the joy of hearing of another's troubles*

as if you owned it; the clear-eyed interloper that would not fall on your sword in obeying commands from those who were themselves unable get the job done.

Welcome to the Brotherhood of World Changers. What took you so long?

56.

On doing the firing

Almost everyone facing the cut on your watch will find their way back into the corporate world. A few brave or desperate souls will attempt the peaks of self-sufficiency. Be gentle.

The economy purrs on and the condemned's economic value must surely be appreciated by someone with a different measure than yours. After all, your current wife is probably also someone's ex?

Recycling the units of production which don't own the means thereof is a necessity – some move upwards, many just sideways, and a few change course completely. Business is dynamic and you are the one stepping on the accelerator. The ride may be too bumpy for some and too exhausting for others. Some will not adapt, others may not want to, and at times there are unforgiveable disasters that require public spectacle.

'It's professional, not personal'; and 'it's fair and reasonable' are the Gog and Magog* of your wrath. Do not prolong the agony of uncertainty. Do the deed yourself. Be honest and humane. Let them go with enough dignity, cash and tools to still sing your praises once they've settled on another perch.

Be especially generous in restructuring – where the business should bear collective punishment for under-performance, but the burden falls uneven on the innocent. You should be marching with them and some of your nine lives would now be missing: there for the grace of the Good Lord, goes I.

---

* *Gog and Magog are two mythical giants protecting the City of London*

57.

THE UNENDING QUEST TO BE RIGHT

Everyone around you have their own personal battles to fight which you may know nothing of. They look at you and wonder if everything is actually as perfect as it looks. It may be so, but there's one battle that is not on their radar, the one that you fight moment to moment, wherein you're tested decision after decision: to be right.

Your judgement carries the entire army. Your pronouncements sways the strategy. Your nod condemns or promotes. Your silence is the dread of misfortune for the listener.

You had better be right. Correct. Every. Single. Time.

This is you quest, your challenge, your journey and your daily tests. Are you good enough? Are you right?

Whatever decisions you make will echo long after you have moved on, as thunder or as earthquakes. You as Captain need to peer into the mist with all available eyes on deck staring in the same direction for clues about the future. You may ask opinions, you may seek advice and you may delegate as much as you want; it is still your call whether to furl the mainsheet open and reach or to reef it in anticipating of deadly gusts. Your call, your responsibility, your watch. It is unending, harsh and vicious if out of control.

Thus sail the ships with the Captains of Industry on the bridge. You too, in the direction to find the port that you chose. It may be a long and hazardous journey and it may bring great satisfaction as well as tales of danger and despair that was overcome. The scars and stories will be hard-earned and the experience beyond what money can buy. Stand straight and true to your calling and steer your course well.

May your mistakes be small and fixable. May your quest be successful.

58.

SUCKING UP

If it goes against your grain, read on.

In one word: Don't. Show respect upwards, sideways and downwards. That's where your politeness ends and your professionalism begins. You cannot and should not depend on the largesse of others and it is dangerous for your career and your self-image to want to get something-for-nothing after ingratiating yourself.

Make it a rule to politely turn down any generosity from sucker-ups, as you do not know what reciprocity may be demanded. You are your own man and you carve the path ahead in your own way. Your luck may steer you into the ambit of the powerful but they serve as waystations for your journey and not ports to latch on to as a parasite.

Sail parallel to that shore and keep a friendly distance. Don't let your desires or wishes show, as these may be baited and you will have a hard time refusing and explaining the hooks dragging you in. Make it your nature to give and share without expecting a return or even gratitude. Your benevolence is only available while you still carry the mortal coil.

Give unexpectedly, graciously and properly to overwhelm the senses. To offer things that money cannot buy is best. Choose scarce, old and unique trinkets for the wealthy and usable, needed real assets for those whom you think are in need. Better still – offer small tokens of well-wishing to those whom you think would appreciate such gestures of care.

Alpha dogs make their own way. You don't sell or trade your independence.

59.

Competing against yourself

He stares back from your shaving mirror. He wakes you up at ungodly hours, jolts your thoughts in the shower and drives you to that congratulatory drink. He is jealous of others and suspicious of most; at best he is an inner voice exhalating sport science Guru Tim Noakes:

> 'Your body will argue that there is no justifiable reason to continue. Your only recourse is to call on your spirit which, fortunately works independently of logic'.

Then he will spit brimstone and ego-dissolving acid when things turn sour. Who are you competing against? Yourself? Are there traces of jealousies of other *Übermenschen* in your emotional mind? And if you are clear from such sin, is it your future or your past self who you are shadowing and trying to beat?

There are many rich veins in Stoicism and some have crossed these pages.

> '*I have often found it strange that every man loves himself more than anyone else and yet values his own opinion of himself less than the opinions others have about him.*'

Thus spoke Marcus Aurelius, Emperor and Stoic philosopher.

Your purpose is inner growth and outer service as a stoic – so it's the future do-gooder that you want to surpass. The ancient Greek philosopher Epictetus said:

> '*Our lack of confidence does not come from difficulty; our difficulty comes from lack of confidence.*'

Man-up a few more degrees, bud. You are always approaching a rising zenith and there's Jacob's ladder right in front of you. These are your steps you're staring up at in the future. You are rising at your own pace, *Chef d'Enterprise,* not competing with anyone, not competing with your current self but doing Citius, Altius, Fortius* for the future business Olympian in you.

---

* *Citius, Altius, Fortius: The Olympic motto; faster, higher, stronger*

60.

LAST WORDS ON COMMON SENSE

The subtitle of these three manuscripts of the unconventional CEO is 'Common Sense'. In an era of cascading opinions, of every blogger posing as an expert, of being confronted by fake everything and with a widespread tendency to hype the marginal stuff, having common sense is a dying attribute.

Think 'grandpa's wisdom' – 'things are what they are, let's not get excited and let's fix it'. It's the almost-true but completely wrong 'ideas' that man-trap the unwary. Three thousand books on my bookshelf and it is still difficult to distil all the wisdom and apply it as common sense.

Harder stuff scratches softer stuff. Wet stuff will rust. Sticky stuff attract critters. Leave it where you found it after borrowing it. These farm lessons are becoming moot as farm kids urbanize.

It is a fact that most Springbok Captains in all our main sports grew up rurally. Things are simple there and are kept simple. Go uncomplicate your stuff. Make things easy to do and to repeat. Spend time on high-value outcomes. Concern yourself with what is under your control. Speak simply. Say what you mean. Treat all with respect. It sounds inane to try and list common-sense things but you will immediately spot likeminded common-sensers and it is a brotherhood of mutual trust.

Clever people can confuse you; wise people won't. Some are brave, others are foolish and fearless. Common sense should help you tell the difference. Some opportunities shine like Venus and others are Venus flytraps. Common sense is an easily learned attribute. These 200 ideas may have triggered the 'of course!' reaction with you; now add a few to your wise-man arsenal.

You will experience your own lessons – do write them down and share them. You will see what you set out to see and reach what you had aimed for. Between Confidence and Common Sense you will make you mark: very high above the waterline and it will be there for all to notice amongst the other great Unconventionals of business.

I am looking forward to pointing that out to my girls one day.

Afterword: does your organization need a CEO?

An adult playing with kids can be the natural leader. Amongst adults he may not be one – and that's the final thought on your Unconventional journey.

If you surround yourself with the kind of talented people that you think you are yourself, the chances are that they will usurp the power and decisions that a normally pyramidical, military hierarchical, closely controlled structure clasps to its breast as if sacred.

If you let go, their creative and competitive juices may flow, decisions taken on initiative and competing visions may dance the Darwin. It should be a golden age where you recruit the best and see them blossom. With time the question might become really interesting; does your Organization still need you as a CEO?

Now you're ready for the Chairmanship. Good luck!